I Made the EARTH

Written by
Shannon Cook

Illustrated by
Richard Watson

An imprint of
END GAME PRESS

I Made the Earth

Wren & Bear Books titles may be purchased in bulk at special discounts for sales promotion, corporate gifts, ministry, fund-raising, or educational purposes. Special editions can also be created to specifications.
For details, contact Special Sales Dept., End Game Press, P.O. Box 206, Nesbit, MS 38651 or info@endgamepress.com.

Visit our website at www.wrenandbearbooks.com

Library of Congress Control Number: 2022939863
ISBN: 978-1-63797-053-9
eBook ISBN: 978-1-63797-054-6

Published in association with Blythe Daniel of The Blythe Daniel Agency, Inc
Cover & Interior Design by TLC Design
Illustrated by Richard Watson, The Bright Agency

Printed in China
10 9 8 7 6 5 4 3 2 1

DEDICATION

For: Anna, Hudson, Nora, and Grady.
While I was reading books to you,
I became a writer.

For: Ryan, my rock and encourager.
This could never have happened
without your support.

To: Calla + Audra
Get outside + enjoy
creation!

So...can you guess what time it is?
It's time for Earth Day fun!

You see the things in this big world?
I made them—every one!

I made the giant whales that swim.

I made the coral reef.

I made
the giant trees
so tall,
And every
tiny leaf.

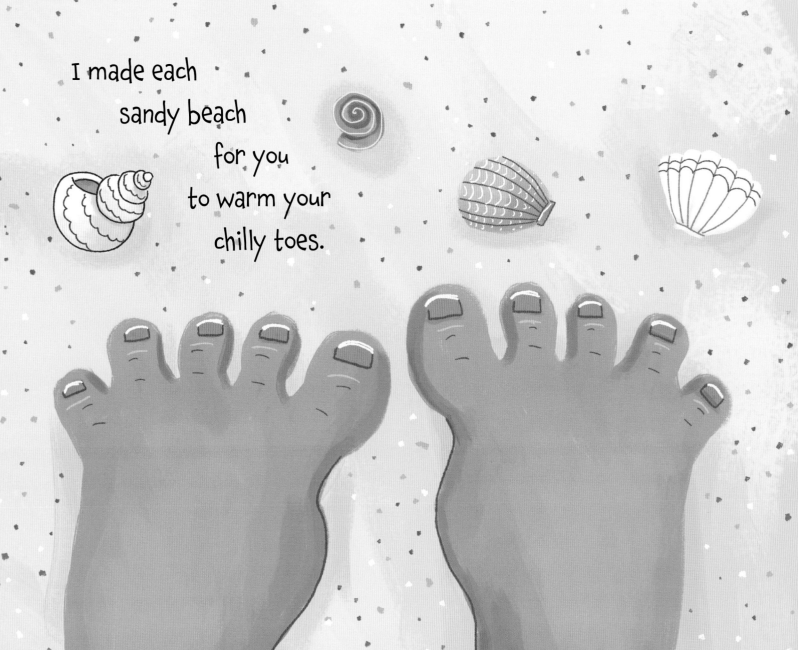

I made each
sandy beach
for you
to warm your
chilly toes.

I made the wind that blows the clouds
And wiggles all the trees.

I made the rain that cools the earth,
Just like a summer breeze.

ALL I ASK
IS TAKE CARE
OF THEM,
PLEASE.

I made the forests, lush and green— Just perfect for a hike.

Or you could have a picnic lunch or ride a mountain bike!

I made each lovely
waterfall,
Some stand
so very high.

I made the silvery moon you see
That lights the darkest sky.

I made the fish so colorful.
Their beauty fills the sea.

I made the cute koala bears
That sleep high in a tree.
I GAVE YOU THESE THINGS SO YOU CAN KNOW ME.

I made each fruit that tastes so good.
They're yummy
and they're sweet.

I also grew your vegetables—

Each artichoke and beet.

I made the tall and wavy grass
Where creatures live and hide.

You'll find brown ants and ladybugs—
Just take a peek inside.

I made the giant panda bears.

They love to munch bamboo.

I made each brightly-colored rose,
And covered them with dew.

I MADE ALL THESE THINGS BECAUSE I LOVE YOU.

I gave this earth to you, My child,
So you could know My heart.

I know that you'll protect this world,
And Earth Day
is a start.

Take care of Earth; please do your best!

And keep this planet free!

EACH TIME YOU CELEBRATE EARTH DAY, YOU'RE CELEBRATING ME.

HERE ARE A FEW WAYS
LITTLE KIDS CAN MAKE A BIG IMPACT.

1. Turn off lights when you leave the room.

2. Pick up trash when you take a walk.

3. Before you throw something away, decide if it can be reused.

4. Make a recycling plan that works for your family.

5. Visit a local zoo or aquarium.
The more you know about animals,
the more you'll want to protect them.

6. Get outside and experience nature!

FIVE FUN FACTS
ABOUT EARTH DAY

1. Earth Day is always celebrated on April 22.

2. The first celebration of Earth Day took place in 1970.

3. Earth Day went global in 1990.

4. Today more than 190 nations celebrate Earth Day.

5. Because of Earth Day, the United States established
   the Environmental Protection Agency (EPA)
   as well as the Clean Air Act, Clean Water Act,
   and The Endangered Species Act.

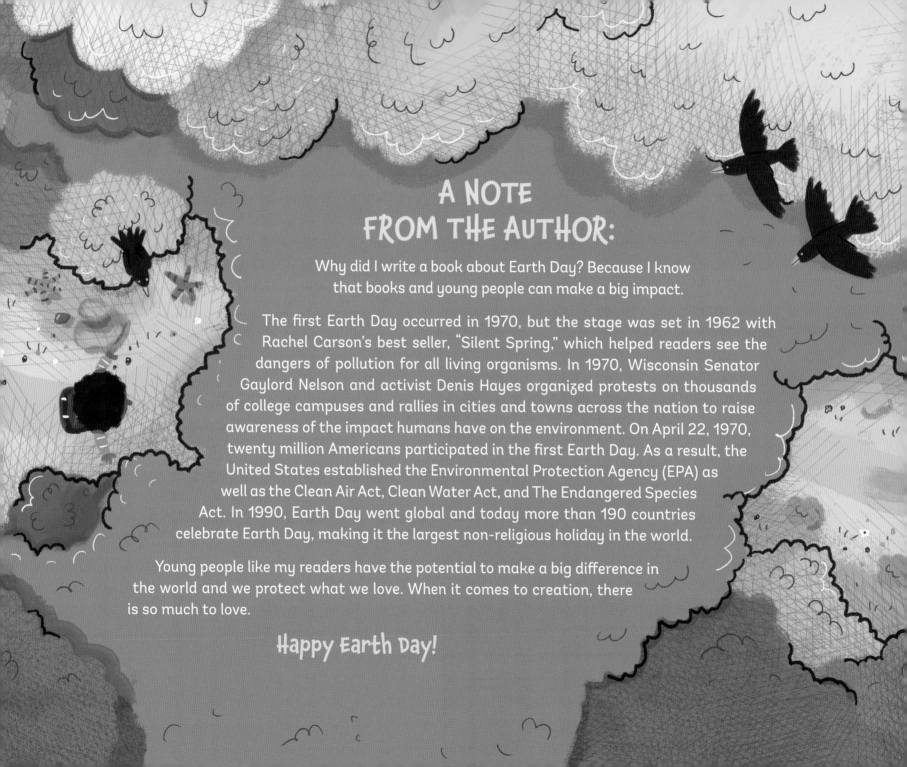

A NOTE FROM THE AUTHOR:

Why did I write a book about Earth Day? Because I know that books and young people can make a big impact.

The first Earth Day occurred in 1970, but the stage was set in 1962 with Rachel Carson's best seller, "Silent Spring," which helped readers see the dangers of pollution for all living organisms. In 1970, Wisconsin Senator Gaylord Nelson and activist Denis Hayes organized protests on thousands of college campuses and rallies in cities and towns across the nation to raise awareness of the impact humans have on the environment. On April 22, 1970, twenty million Americans participated in the first Earth Day. As a result, the United States established the Environmental Protection Agency (EPA) as well as the Clean Air Act, Clean Water Act, and The Endangered Species Act. In 1990, Earth Day went global and today more than 190 countries celebrate Earth Day, making it the largest non-religious holiday in the world.

Young people like my readers have the potential to make a big difference in the world and we protect what we love. When it comes to creation, there is so much to love.

Happy Earth Day!

ABOUT THE AUTHOR

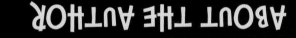

SHANNON COOK is a mom, blogger, and former teacher. She also loves books for holidays and seasons. Since her husband has been a leader in green energy for over 20 years, she and her kids have a special place in their hearts for Earth Day. When she couldn't find any books about God and Earth Day, she decided to write one. This is her debut, but she also writes middle grade historical fiction. Shannon, Ryan, and their four children live near Columbus, Ohio, and their house is filled with books.

ABOUT THE ILLUSTRATOR

RICHARD WATSON has illustrated many children's books including the hilarious James Patterson Dog Diaries series, written by Junior, the first dog author to top the New York Times Bestseller list. He mainly sits underneath the stairs drawing stuff and enjoys guitars, long walks in the woods, and spooky things. Richard is represented by the Bright Agency.

26 Then God said, "Let us make mankind in our image, in our likeness, so that they may rule over the fish in the sea and the birds in the sky, over the livestock and all the wild animals, and over all the creatures that move along the ground."

27 So God created mankind in his own image, in the image of God he created them; male and female he created them.

28 God blessed them and said to them, "Be fruitful and increase in number; fill the earth and subdue it. Rule over the fish in the sea and the birds in the sky and over every living creature that moves on the ground."

29 Then God said, "I give you every seed-bearing plant on the face of the whole earth and every tree that has fruit with seed in it. They will be yours for food.

30 And to all the beasts of the earth and all the birds in the sky and all the creatures that move along the ground—everything that has the breath of life in it—I give every green plant for food." And it was so.

31 God saw all that he had made, and it was very good…

GENESIS 1:26-31, NIV